We were there

THE 1970s

Rosemary Rees

Heinemann Library,
an imprint of Heinemann Publishers (Oxford) Ltd,
Halley Court, Jordan Hill, Oxford, OX2 8EJ

OXFORD LONDON EDINBURGH
MADRID PARIS ATHENS BOLOGNA
MELBOURNE SYDNEY AUCKLAND
SINGAPORE TOKYO IBADAN
NAIROBI GABORONE HARARE
PORTSMOUTH NH (USA)

First published 1993
93 94 95 96 10 9 8 7 6 5 4 3 2 1

British Library Cataloguing in Publication Data
is available on request from the British Library.

ISBN 0 431 07328 7

Designed by Philip Parkhouse
Printed and bound in China

Acknowledgements
The author and publisher would like to thank the following
for permission to reproduce photographs:
The Advertising Archives p. 20
Arcaid/Richard Einzig p. 6
Barnaby's Picture Library p. 5
BFI Stills p. 16; BBC p. 18; Collections/Brian Shuel p. 7
Camera Press pp. 23, 27; Robert Harding p. 30
Hulton-Deutsch Collection p. 22; Denise Kent p. 29
Judith Maguire p. 28; Robert Opie p. 17
Popperfoto p. 8; Syndication International Ltd p. 19
Topham Picture Source pp. 9, 12, 13, 14, 15
Stephen Vickers pp. 21, 25

Cover photograph: Aspect Picture Library

The author and publisher would like to thank all of
the people who contributed memories to this book.

Note to the reader
In this book there are some words in the text
which are printed in **bold type**. This shows that
the words are listed in the glossary on page 31.
The glossary gives a brief explanation of words
that may be new to you.

Contents

Home 1

Many town houses like this were built in the 1970s. Rosemary Dawson and her husband moved into this house in 1974.

Rosemary Dawson remembers how she felt about the house at the time.

We had to move, and this was a good house in a lot of ways. But I didn't want to live there. It was not very well **designed** for a mum who had young children. I remember thinking that it was probably designed by a man. This was because the ground floor had the garage built into the house, and a **cloakroom** and a **utility room**. That was all. It was very neat to look at,

having the garage built into the house. It was very useful having the washing machine in the utility room, well away from the rest of the house. It was also nice to have the living room on the first floor, because you had much nicer views. But it was a really bad idea to have the kitchen on the first floor too. In our old house, if I was in the kitchen the boys could play in the garden and be near me. I could keep an eye on them. In this house they were a whole set of stairs and a corridor away.

Margaret Hudson had a brother who went off to share a flat with some friends.

Simon went off to live with these friends in a flat in Sheffield. When they rented the flat they were told that they could decorate it, if they wanted to. I saw the flat before they moved in, it was all white walls, with flower wallpaper in the bedrooms, although they were a bit dirty. He and the others decorated it in what were called 'psychadelic' colours and patterns.

It was all wild swirls in really bright colours. It really hurt your eyes as you went into every room. The most amazing colours went into the paint on the woodwork too, really bright green and yellow next to each other. This was just what he had wanted to do to his bedroom at home, but our mum had always said no. I thought it was wonderful, mum just shuddered, and said she couldn't see how they ever got to sleep in rooms that bright!

In the 1970s many young people decorated their rooms in a way that was called 'psychadelic'. There were lots of bright, swirling colours.

Home 2

Not everyone thought 'psychadelic' decorations were a good idea. This kitchen has some bright colours, and lots of space. Bare bricks painted white were very popular.

Jane Gross and her husband bought their first house in the 1970s.

In the late 1970s we bought our first house, Paul had his first job. I can't remember any new labour saving machines for the kitchen, but people seemed to me to spend more time in the kitchen. Cooking became **trendy**. People stopped seeing cooking as something that you did because you had to eat. They stopped seeing eating as something that interrupted all sorts of fun things. They began to see food as fun. We had dinner parties almost every weekend, and so did our friends. You began to see more unusual food in the supermarkets, and there were shops which sold special spices and herbs. Suddenly there were lots of cookery books in the shops, cookery magazines on the shelves, and cookery programmes on the TV. Complicated French recipes were popular, and Italian ones. I remember lasagne was seen as a very unusual dish to cook!

Paul Shuter's mother, Joan, can remember how people felt about decimalization.

It was all very confusing. People didn't feel prepared for the changeover. I was OK, because I was good at maths, but other people, especially old people, found it difficult. Very few shops showed charts of prices in both sets of money. One day the food was priced in old money, the next day it was new money. Frank, my husband, was a postmaster, he had to go to learn to use the new money. The postmasters had to play shops with toy new money, to get used to it. Someone had decided it was easier to teach them how to use the new money only using a few coins, so they were only allowed to give change using 2p and 1p coins. This meant that to give 6p change as 5p and 1p was 'wrong'!

This supermarket helped its customers to cope with decimalization. It had a sign to show prices in decimal and in old money.

School 1

British money changed in 1971. Instead of using 'old money' (pounds, shillings and pence) children were taught to use 'new money' (pounds and new pence).

Rosamund Forbes was taught to use 'new money' in school.

We were taught how to use new money when I was about ten. The teacher kept telling us that it was going to be really easy, much better than old money. In old money you had twelve pennies in a shilling, and twenty shillings in a pound. You also had odd coins, like sixpence, which was six pennies, and half a crown, which was two shillings and sixpence. The new money was working on just pence and pounds. There were a hundred pence in a pound, and no odd coin, so it was supposed to be easier. I suppose it was, but I was used to the old money, so the new money seemed hard. I hated having to do 'conversion' work where you changed an amount in old money, say two shillings, into new money. I found it was quite easy to learn once you had the real money and had to go out and spend it, then it all seemed sensible.

Children on an Outward Bound course. Children had to do several outdoor tasks, including walking a long distance and camping out.

Ursula Gibbons' class went on an adventure holiday in 1975.

We went canoeing in the River Wye for a week. We camped, boys and girls in separate tents, at a place called Symonds Yatt. It was quite fun camping, although it was cold. We went canoeing each day with the instructors. We had to wear helmets, to make sure we didn't hurt our heads if we fell into the water or against the bank. We also had to wear **life jackets** to be safe, even if we could swim.

It was fun, but quite difficult. It was easy canoeing **downstream**, because the water helped you to go along. It was much harder going **upstream**, because the water kept pushing you back, and you had to paddle really hard. I was so slow at going upstream that I got left behind, and everyone had to wait for me to catch up. In the end they tied my canoe to one of the instructors' canoes. This meant that I was towed up the river, and although I still paddled, I could not get left behind!

School 2

Thomas Hughes at his playgroup in Wakefield in 1974. He is the one in the blue jumper and shorts on the left of the picture. His best friend, Timmy, is standing next to him.

Rosemary Dawson remembers her son going to playgroup in Wakefield.

When we were living in Wakefield, Thomas went to **playgroup** every morning. He went to the one in the picture for two mornings a week, and to one on the other side of Wakefield for the other three mornings. This was his favourite playgroup. It was in the **basement** of a church hall, and you had to have the lights on all the time, it was pretty gloomy. But it was very friendly and there weren't too many rules. His favourite game was to cycle around first thing in the morning, on a small tricycle and deliver the little plastic **cartons** of milk to everyone to have for their drink. One morning a photographer was coming to take everyone's photo, so Thomas wasn't allowed to give out the milk in case it got spilt on the children's smart clothes. He was very angry, and thought it was all the photographer's fault! He refused to be in the photo.

Rosemary Dawson went to watch the Nativity Play in Hadstock, Essex in 1971.

This play was put on by the Playgroup while we were living near Hadstock. The mums from the villages around Hadstock took it in turns to deliver and pick up the children who went there. Everyone worked very hard to practice for the Nativity Play and to put on a really good show for all the people who came. The costumes were all made by the ladies who were in charge of the playgroup, and I think they wrote the play too. Some children were very nervous about appearing. But Geraint wasn't at all nervous. He was very excited about it, and loved being up on stage in front of everyone. It would not have mattered if the kids had made any mistakes, but I don't think that they did. I do remember that afterwards we were all very proud of them. They were very proud of themselves too, even the children who had been scared before they went on.

Geraint Hughes was a king in his playschool Nativity Play in 1971. Geraint is the king in the middle of the three kings.

Work 1

An oil rig in the North Sea. In the 1970s the North Sea was drilled for oil for the first time. The oil rigs needed workers. People moved to Scotland to work on them.

Marie Thiel's son was a diver and a pilot, and thought about going to work on the rigs.

Dave was a good diver and a good pilot, and people who could do these things were needed to work on the rigs. Several of his friends were working in the North Sea. I remember that there were lots of adverts in the paper for people to move to Scotland and work on the rigs. The oil **companies** were offering people a lot of money to go to work for them – people could earn more on the rigs than anywhere else, even people who were doing ordinary jobs, like the cooking and the cleaning. The companies were paying the extra money because of the hard work and the inconvenience. If there was bad weather you could get stuck on the rig during your time off. People who dived and worked the machinery were also paid more because the work was dangerous. Dave was asked to work on the rigs. I was very scared that he would go, but he didn't in the end.

During the miners' strike of 1972 there were lots of power cuts. People had to work by gas or oil lamps, or even by candlelight.

Jane Gross did her homework by candlelight.

During the miners' strike we had a lot of **power cuts**. Some people had houses where everything worked off electricity, even the kettles and cookers. We were often told when the cuts would be. You cooked when the power was on, even if it wasn't a mealtime! We were lucky, we had a coal **stove** that you could boil the kettle on . So all we had to worry about was lighting. This was a worry, though, because we didn't have any lamps.

Some people had gas, oil or paraffin lamps, but all we had were candles. It was OK at first, but then the shops started running low on candles, and would only sell a few at a time. So we could not use many. We all lived in the room that the stove was in, all the time. By end of the strike we used only one or two candles to light the room. I got first turn with them, because I had homework to do, then other people had a go, to read! We all gave in homework with candle wax all over it.

Work 2

These people are shearing sheep, cutting the fleece off from the skin. It was just like having a haircut, and didn't hurt the sheep. It was done every year.

Jane Gross lived in Devon. Some of her friends lived on farms.
There were lots of ways that farming in Devon didn't change at all really, from the early 1960s when I moved there, to the later 1970s when I left. You still saw tractors and balers at harvest time, sheep still had to be sheared each year. My friends who lived on farms worked very hard on the farm before and after school. Most of the boys went on to be farmers, and the girls went on to marry farmers.

There were some things that changed. The father of one of my friends found that it made him more money to rent his field out to campers than to grow corn on it. Lots of other farmers started to do this. When they were talking about the crops they were planting for the next year they would often say that one of their fields would be used for 'growing grockles' (the word we used for holidaymakers). Some of them did more and more of this, and less and less actual farming.

An insurance company in the 1970s. Men and women worked together in the same office. The secretaries were in a separate room called the typing pool.

Paul Shuter went to work in an insurance company in the 1970s.
The building I worked in was huge. It had its own system of telephones to speak to people in other parts of the office, as well as for speaking to people in other places. In our office you never saw the secretaries. They were all in a big room on another floor. When I started I had to write out the letters I wanted to send, so my boss could check them before they were typed. Later on I just rang up the **typing pool** on the telephone **switchboard** and **dictated** the letters that I wanted typed. Then, usually an hour or so later, my letters would be brought up to me by one of the boys who spent all day delivering letters from the typing pool. I went there once, to find out what had happened to some letters I had dictated. It was huge, with the desks in rows, and all the secretaries typing on electric machines, with headphones on. They were listening to the taped letters, I suppose.

Spare Time 1

The poster advertising the film 'Star Wars', which was made by Stephen Spielberg, used special effects never seen before.

Ursula Gibbons went to the cinema a lot in the 1970s.

In 1975–6 I went to the cinema a lot. This was because my boyfriend was the son of the manageress of our cinema! He and I were allowed to go in free. The films I remember most were about disasters and how people escaped from them. We saw several, one after the other, they all came out at about the same time. One was 'Airplane', and another one, about a fire in a tall building, was 'Towering Inferno'.

Judith Maguire went to see 'Star Wars' when she was living in Liverpool.

You had to queue for ages to get in. We were worried that we would be too far back in the queue to get in. But we did, and the cinema was packed full of people, and very hot. It was exciting, I enjoyed the fight with 'light sabre' weapons the best. Star Wars became a playground game. People kept saying the phrase "May the Force be with you", which was used a lot in the film.

No. 466 DECEMBER 9th. 1972   THURSDAYS.   4p

Jackie

HAPPY BIRTHDAY DONNY!

***Jackie* was one of the most popular teenage magazines of the 1970s. It often had a pop star's photo on the cover.**

Jane Gross read *Jackie* regularly.

I really enjoyed *Jackie*. I had it on order at the newspaper shop, so that I didn't miss an issue! It had articles about pop stars, and almost always a pop star on the cover, but it also had lots of other things. It had a letter each week, written by a girl called Sue Arnold (she is now a journalist). Then she was only young, and her column was full of things about having spots, and the boy she liked not liking her, and how her parents drove her mad.

Kate Upcott read *Jackie* and *Princess*, another comic for girls.

I used to go to the newspaper stand on the corner to buy a comic most weeks. I would get *Jackie* or *Princess*. I used to think that *Jackie* was a better comic, but *Princess* had really good free gifts, like plastic bracelets and pretty combs to hold up long hair. So I chose my comic by what the free gift was. The best thing to read in both of the magazines were the serials, the stories that went on week after week.

Spare Time 2

A photo from the TV programme called 'The Magic Roundabout'. It was very popular with young children.

Jane Gross watched 'The Magic Roundabout' even though she was a teenager.

'The Magic Roundabout' was the TV programme that everyone in our **sixth form** watched. If you didn't watch that and another, much more grown up programme called 'Monty Python's Flying Circus', you had nothing to talk about the next day, because everyone was talking about these programmes. I'm not sure why 'The Magic Roundabout' was such a big thing,

perhaps it was to do with the rabbit in it called Dylan, who was a very 1970s **hippie** sort of rabbit, who wandered about in a vague sort of way saying that things were "Cool, man". The puppet on a spring was called Zebedee, and he went "Boiing" all over the place, and that was something that kept coming into conversations. Also, it ended with the **phrase**, "Time for bed, said Zebedee" which kept coming into conversations too. The shaggy dog was called Dougal.

Judith Maguire used to watch 'Tiswas' when she lived in Liverpool.

'Tiswas' used to be on ITV on a Saturday morning. There were lots of different, crazy things going on, all at once. There were cartoons, interviews with pop stars, and competitions. It was on at the same time as 'Saturday Morning Swap Shop' on BBC. We used to change channels from time to time, to catch the best bits of each of them. What I liked best about 'Tiswas' was the part where people were shut into a cage and had water or horrid slime, I can't remember which, poured all over them. The funny thing is that I can't remember what they did to get put in there at all, just that every week it happened to someone! There was also a person called The Phantom Flan Thrower, who came along at odd moments and pushed a plate of that squishy cream into people faces, or thow it so that it hit them somewhere or other. That was funny too.

A photograph of some of the 'Tiswas' team. They have had pies thrown at them by the Phantom Flan Thrower, who is at the back dressed in black.

Spare Time 3

Spectrum Latest!

Crazy clogs and zany platforms! Weird wild shapes and outrageous colours. They're the latest maddest offering in the Spectrum range. On the left, Doozie at £6.50.

On top, Mata at £5.25 and on the right, Hari from £5.25. Nearest shop? Write to Clarks (Dept. ZL 11), Street, Somerset, and ask for a **Spectrum** style leaflet. *by Clarks*

Similar styles available in the Republic of Ireland. Write to Clarks, Dundalk for details and prices.

Platform shoes were popular in the 1970s. They got taller and taller, until it was hard to balance in them!

Jane Gross wore platform shoes and boots.

Platform shoes started out quite low, and we all bought them. Lots of shoes then were made from **suede**. I had a pair of pink suede platform shoes which I loved, they were surprisingly comfortable to walk in! But as the shoes got higher, they got much more difficult to walk in. Skirts were still very short at the time, and platform boots that came to just above the knee became the thing that we all wanted.

Boots like this in real suede cost far too much, so I bought a pair in pretend suede. They were a lot cheaper, but they had a horrid smell, which never went away. They were black, and I thought they were very smart, despite the smell, but they were so high that they were very hard to walk in. We lived in Devon, which is very hilly. The first night I had them I went to a disco with my friends and we nearly missed the bus because I could hardly walk down the steep hill to the bus stop!

Stephen Vickers and his friends, celebrating becoming teachers! In the late 1970 skirts went from being very short to being very long.

Jane Gross had to pack away her mini skirts.

After mini skirts we wore 'midi' skirts, which were about six inches below the knee. But they were not really very popular, because it wasn't easy to look good in them. Then there was a craze for velvet, especially crushed velvet, or 'panne' velvet, as it was called. This was far more stretchy and comfortable than real velvet, and was easier to clean. You could get it in all sorts of colours, like gold, purple, red and dark green. When I left the sixth form, in 1976, I made myself a dark green panne velvet dress for the party they were giving for the leavers. It took a long time to make, but it looked lovely. I was very proud of it. The material was actually curtain material, not dress material, but that year everyone was wearing it! Even some of the boys wore panne velvet long-sleeved tee shirts, although only the brave ones, who wanted to seem very fashionable. Almost all of us wore flared jeans.

Holidays 1

Concorde, the first ever supersonic aeroplane. It made crossing the Atlantic Ocean to America really fast. But it was very expensive to run.

Not everyone wanted Concorde. Margaret Hudson remembers how people worried about it.

The local TV news reported on the designing and testing of Concorde at Filton, near Bristol. The people in charge of the design were really keen on Concorde, but lots of the local people thought that it was a very bad thing. They were convinced that it would be bad for the health of the people who were passengers on it, and that it would be even worse for the people who lived near the airport that it used. When Concorde was due to be tested there were old people in the **district** who went and spent the day in their **air-raid shelter** in the garden, left over from the Second World War, because they were convinced that when the plane went faster than sound all their windows would break, and maybe their eardrums! I remember Brian Trubshaw, who did the first test flight of the plane, saying on TV how good it had been.

Foreign holidays became cheaper in the 1970s. There were 'package holidays' which arranged travel and a place to stay all in one go. Spain was very popular.

Paul Shuter went on holiday to Spain with his parents and his girlfriend in 1975.

Holidays abroad were just becoming something that you could afford. We didn't go by plane, that was still a very expensive way to travel. We went by MotorRail. You bought a ticket from British Rail for you and your car as far as the border between France and Spain. Then, at a place called Narbonne, you and the car left the train, and you drove the rest of the way to where you were staying. We were staying in a village in an area that was just beginning to build lots of hotels for people to come on holiday. The village was a fishing village then, with some holiday flats. Hotels were being built in lots of villages, there were half-finished buildings everywhere. Most of them were being built by a building firm called *Joe Ripoll*, so we used to have competitions about how many Joe Ripoll building works we could spot in a car journey!

Holidays 2

Geraint and Thomas Hughes, on holiday in Scotland. In the 1970s Scotland was a very popular place to go on holiday.

Rosemary Dawson went to Scotland on holiday several times.

I think this holiday was in 1976 or 1977, I'm not sure which. I am sure that it was the holiday where it rained and rained, all the time. Luckily we were not camping! We were staying in a flat where were had to do all the cooking and cleaning for ourselves. We didn't let the rain stop us going out. We went out and visited a lot of places, and did a lot of walking.

Because it was so wet and miserable we did things to cheer ourselves up. Because we were on holiday we felt we had to go out to see things and places. This was quite fun.

We decided that we would not do so much cooking for ourselves. We all like food, but we did not enjoy cooking it. Our treat to cheer ourselves up was to have lots of really nice meals out, in lots of different places. The rain and the eating out are the things that I remember most.

Stephen Vickers went camping in Scotland in the 1970s. He took this photo of some of his friends relaxing in the grounds of the campsite.

Becky Vickers, Stephen's wife, remembers the holiday well.

There seemed to be two sorts of people that went camping in Scotland. There were people like us, young people, in their twenties, who had very little money, and only very simple camping and cooking equipment. Then there were people who were in their fifties, and who were much more organized. They had caravans, or very grand tents. They brought an amazing amount of stuff with them: folding tables and chairs, proper china plates, **cutlery** and tablecloths. They had all sorts of different cooking stoves and lamps for the tents at night, and they cooked really complicated meals, just as if they were at home. Almost everyone was British. On this holiday it rained, of course. There were also lots and lots of **midges**, which bit Stephen the most. We covered ourselves in **insect repellant**, but they still bit us, Stephen swelled up around the eyes. The bites really itched!

Special Days 1

A street party to celebrate the Queen's Silver Jubilee. This meant that she had been queen for twenty five years. All sorts of people celebrated in lots of different ways.

Ursula Gibbons went to a Ball at Sandhurst Military College.

I was very excited about going to the **ball**. I had a lovely long dress that was pale blue. We went by train. It was full of girls of about eighteen, carrying big suitcases with their dresses in, all with their hair done and make-up on, all feeling very nervous! We watched parades before the dancing. When I got home my lovely dress was black all around the bottom with polish that had come off the soldiers' shiny boots.

Becky Vickers celebrated in a very different way.

We had a party on the green in the middle of our housing estate in Leamington. There were lots of Italian and Indian people in our street, so we had lots of different food, including a huge Union Jack made out of rice which was coloured red, white and blue. We also had curry, pasta and sausage rolls. The children dressed up, and we played lots of games, including a prize for the best decorated bike!

Kath Donovan watched Virginia Wade win.

It was really exciting. It seemed as if the whole of the country was watching, and wishing that Virginia Wade would win. She had been trying to win at Wimbledon for a long time, and lots of people thought that she was too old to have a chance in 1977. It seemed like it was her last chance to win. It had been a very long time since an English woman had won the singles at Wimbledon.

No-one really expected that she would win, but we all really wanted her to. As we saw that she could win we got more and more excited. When she played the winning shot we went wild! It was just such a good thing for her to win, because she seemed such a nice person when you read about her in the papers. It was also such a good thing that someone from England won in 1977, because it was the year of the Queen's Silver Jubilee, and it was another way of celebrating it.

Virgina Wade won the women's singles tennis championship at Wimbledon in 1977.

Special Days 2

A birthday party at Judith's house in the 1970s.

Judith Maguire remembers her birthday parties in the 1970s.
For our birthday parties we were allowed to invite a few friends. The parties were always on the nearest Saturday afternoon to your birthday. Everyone came to the party in their best clothes. You always wore your best clothes to birthday parties, and you were always told to be careful to keep them clean. You always ended up wiping chocolate and other stuff down it at some point though!

We had tea first at our parties. The tea was crisps, sandwiches, little cakes, sausages rolls and the big birthday cake. You got fizzy drinks too. Then we played party games. The games I remember were Pass the Parcel, Musical Chairs, Statues, and Blind Man's Buff. I enjoyed my parties, but I wanted to play with the presents, too. So part of me wanted the birthday to go on for ever, and part of me wanted it to stop so that I would be able to play with the presents!

Denise Kent remembers her wedding, in Harlow in Essex.

My wedding was a fairly quiet one. Not a big traditional wedding in a church. The ceremony was in a register office, but I still wanted a long white dress, bridesmaids and flowers.

My sisters and I spent quite a bit of time choosing the right colour eyeshadows and nail varnish. I think I wore pale green eyeshadow and orangey nail varnish to match my flowers! The night before the wedding the three of us slept with big sponge rollers in our hair. You see, we had such straight hair and we desperately tried to make it curly. As you can see from the picture we weren't very successful. The morning of the wedding was full of excitement and noise. I think there were nine of us trying to use the bathroom at the same time!

Right up until the car arrived, my sisters and I were still plucking our eyebrows, and adding a bit more lip gloss. At last we drove off and I had a lovely, but freezing cold, wedding day.

Denise Kent on her wedding day in December 1977.

Special Days 3

The Death Mask of the Egyptian Pharoah, Tutankhamun. The treasures found in Tutankhamun's tomb were lent to the British Museum for an Exhibition in 1972.

Paul Shuter went to see the Exhibition at the British Museum.
I went up to London for the day with my mum. We started queuing at 10.30am. The queue went round three sides of the Museum. As we got near to the front gates I felt that at last we were nearly there. Then we saw that the queue did not go across the front yard in a straight line. It zigzagged backwards and forwards at least ten times!! I remember wondering if it was worth going on queuing. We decided to stay, and mum went off to get us a drink and some lunch to eat in the queue. We were among the last of the people to get in for the day. I think we got in at about 5.30pm!! You were still in queues and slow moving lines to look at the treasures. I don't remember many of the things now, but I still remember the face mask from Tutankhamun's **sarcophagus** really well. The gold and other colours really glowed, and it looked like the face of a real person.

Glossary

air-raid shelter during the Second World War (1939-45) Britain was bombed by the Germans. The bombing raids were called air raids. Some people hid in underground stations during air raids, many people built air-raid shelters under the ground in their back gardens.

ball a very grand dance, where everyone has to dress up.

basement the part of a building that is under the ground.

cartons cardboard containers, often for milk, juice or ice cream.

cloakroom a downstairs room to keep coats in. They often have toilets and washbasins in them too.

companies the people who work together to make money out of something. Big oil companies are Esso and Shell.

cutlery knives, forks and spoons.

decimalization when we changed from using pounds, shillings and pence (old money) to using decimal money (new money).

designed planned, made to suit someone's needs.

dictated words said out loud to a person, or tape recorder, for writing out later.

district a place.

downstream going along a stream or river the way the water flows.

hippie a person who wore bright clothes, believed in peace, did not believe in owning much.

insect repellent a cream which stops insects biting you.

life jackets jackets that help you to float in the water.

midges mosquitoes, small insects which like damp weather and biting people.

oil rig a place which is set up in the sea to drill for oil under the sea bed.

phrase group of words.

platform shoe a shoe which has got extra pieces on the bottom to make it taller.

playgroup a place where children who are too young for school can go to play together.

postmaster someone who runs a post office.

power cuts when the electricity stops working.

psychadelic very bright and loud. Lots of different colours.

sarcophagus stone coffin which is usually decorated.

sixth form the last two years before you leave secondary school, when you are seventeen and eighteen.

stove cooker.

suede a soft leather, which has a rough surface.

switchboard the place which works all the telephone lines. Some buildings have their own switchboard, just for inside the building.

trendy fashionable.

typing pool a big room where all the office secretaries worked

upstream going along a stream or river, in the opposite direction to the way the water is flowing.

utility room a room for the noisy kitchen machines, like the washing machine, the drying machine, and sometimes the dishwasher.

Index